CHIEFTAINS AND PRINCES

A POWER IN THE LAND OF WALES

Charles Kightly

CONTENTS

Above: *A cast of the great seal, 1205-06, of Llywelyn ab Iorwerth - Llywelyn the Great (d. 1240). (By permission of the National Museum of Wales).*

A POWER IN THE LAND OF WALES

Human beings have continuously occupied Wales for some 12,000 years, and for about half that time have exercised ever-increasing influence on its environment. To an extent not always fully recognized, the Welsh landscape is the product of human activity. The real 'makers of wales', of course, were the countless generations of ordinary men and women who farmed, worked and dwelt in the land. Yet until we consider very recent history, such people remain shadowy figures, unsung and largely anonymous. Welsh history, rather, is dominated by the ruling elite: the chieftains and princes, warlords, nobles, squires and industrialists who wielded power in and over the land.

They are remembered because they alone possessed the resources - such as wealth and the control of labour - to create enduring symbols of their power. It was they who commissioned fortresses and great country houses, to control and impress subjects or rivals. Splendid possessions proclaimed their status in life, and elaborate monuments perpetuated their memory after death. When history came to be written, it was written for and about them: bards sang their deeds and lineage, chroniclers recorded their conquests and setbacks, while painters and sculptors reproduced their appearance for posterity.

Though 'chieftains and princes' constituted only a tiny minority of the population, it was they who stamped their personalities and preoccupations most strongly on the built monuments of Wales, and on the artefacts and manuscripts in Welsh museums and libraries. Necessarily partial and one-sided though it is, the story revealed by such symbols of power is the one this book attempts to trace.

Above Right: Perhaps the most celebrated of all Wales's chieftains and princes, famed in legend, and certainly one of the most enduring, is King Arthur. This fourteenth-century manuscript illustration shows Arthur arriving at Caerleon, where according to tradition the king held court (By permission of the British Library, Ms. Egerton 3028, f. 42).

Left: Castles frequently dominate the mountainous skyline of Wales, standing as symbols of the power wielded by generations of chieftains and princes. Here, at Castell Dinas Brân, Llangollen, Denbighshire, the masonry remains were probably built just before 1270, by Madog, prince of this part of Powys. The medieval builders, however, not only took advantage of the natural defences afforded by the precipitous hilltop location, but also those created by a much earlier power in the land, for the castle stands within the ramparts of an Iron Age hillfort (By courtesy of the Wales Tourist Board).

STONE AGE NOMADS

A fragment of a jaw, dating from around 230,000 B.C., recovered from Pontnewydd cave, Denbighshire. Its owner, hailed as 'the first Welshman', was a young adult, probably aged about twelve years old (By permission of the National Museum of Wales).

The first humans probably appeared in what is now Wales about a quarter of a million years ago, when Britain was still joined to Europe in a single land mass and partly covered by glacial ice sheets. Its first visitors were small groups of Neanderthal hunters, wandering vast territories on the fringe of the habitable world: their numbers were small - probably never more than fifty in 'Wales' at any one time - and their presence impermanent, for whenever the glaciers advanced the land was left unpeopled for tens of thousands of years.

Thus the traces of these 'Old Stone Age' nomads are scanty, confined to discoveries in the caves where they sheltered, and processed the animals they killed or scavenged. One such, Pontnewydd cave in Denbighshire, has produced teeth dating from around 230,000 B.C., the earliest human remains yet found in Wales. But not until some 200,000 years later - by which time the Neanderthals had been superseded by the ancestors of modern man - does any indication of leadership or status appear.

about **230,000 B.C.**	Old Stone Age. Earliest evidence of man in Wales.
about **230,000 - 10,000 B.C.**	Intermittent human occupation during intervals between glaciations.
about **26,000 B.C.**	Ritual burial of 'chieftain' in Paviland Cave.
about **20,000 - 18,000 B.C.**	Maximum spread of ice sheets. Humans driven out.
about **10,000 B.C.**	Ice in final retreat. Continuous habitation of Wales begins.
about **8,500 - 4,500 B.C.**	Middle Stone Age. Much of land covered by forest.
about **4,000 - 3,500 B.C.**	New Stone Age. Arrival of first farmers. Land clearance begins. Communal tombs built.
about **3,000 - 2,750 B.C.**	Clearance of uplands begins. Stone circles and alignments appear.

THE RED LADY OF PAVILAND

Our evidence is the famous 'Red Lady of Paviland', discovered (and misidentified as a Roman woman) in a cave on the Gower coast in 1822. In fact, the 'Lady' was a man aged about 25, and some 5 feet 7 inches (1.7m) tall. He had been ceremonially buried about 26,000 B.C., accompanied by gifts of perforated sea shells and apparently dressed in clothes decorated with mammoth-ivory adornments. His remains were thickly coated in blood-red powder, perhaps symbolizing a hoped-for rebirth. The care taken with his ritual burial must surely indicate that he was a person of some status. Indeed, this point is echoed by similarly-dated burials in shell and ivory bedecked garments found in Russia and Italy. Perhaps the Gower 'Lady' was even a 'chieftain', though the basis of his status - whether strength, cunning, or magical power - remains a mystery.

An imaginative reconstructon drawing of the burial of the 'Red Lady' in Paviland cave on the Gower peninsula. Great care was exercised during the interment of a young man. His body was thickly coated in red ochre and bedecked with sea-shells and clothes decorated with mammoth-ivory adornments, perhaps symbolizing his status both in life and death (By permission of the National Museum of Wales).

Some sixteen millennia after his death, around 10,000 B.C., the glacial ice retreated for the last time, and permanent human occupation of 'Wales' began. In a rapidly improving climate, shrubs and then trees also recolonized the land, and by about 5,500 B.C. much of Wales was cloaked in woodland. The 'Middle Stone Age' hunter-gatherers who inhabited it have left little evidence of their presence save temporary occupation sites. Recently, however, archaeologists discovered a remarkable set of footprints miraculously preserved in the mud of the Usk estuary. A six foot (1.8m) man, another adult and a child had walked this way about 5,000 B.C.

Left: These footprints show that at least three people walked across the mud of the Usk estuary over 6,500 years ago. Whether they were out hunting or fishing we do not know, but it seems likely that they belonged to one of the bands of Middle Stone Age hunter-gatherers who began to take advantage of the rich natural resources available in Wales following the final retreat of the last ice sheets. Elsewhere, evidence of their occupation is recognized from the tiny flint tools they left behind. Here, however, these footprints have been remarkably preserved in the estuarine clays which fringe the river Severn, capturing forever the record of a single expedition (By permission of the National Museum of Wales).

Left: The stark silhouette of Pentre Ifan burial chamber on the edge of the Preseli Hills, Pembrokeshire. To raise such a massive monument would have required a concerted communal effort, perhaps undertaken to proclaim the community's power in the land as well as to commemorate its ancestors.

Below: A stone axe from Aberavon, near Port Talbot. Communal monuments required land free from trees and scrub; so too did the farming of crops and animals. The main tools used for clearing trees were smoothly polished stone axes, wedged in wooden hafts. Such tools are likely to have been highly prized and the loss of this axe, with its birch-wood handle still intact, may have occasioned the owner some distress (By permission of the National Museum of Wales).

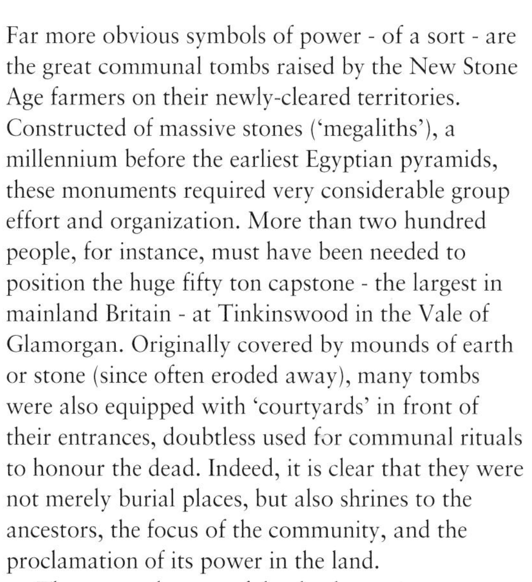

Two stone axes made of volcanic rock from the Graig Lwyd 'factory', Conwy. That on the left is an unfinished 'rough out' from the 'factory', and the finely polished example on the right was found at Rhosybol, Anglesey. Analysis of such axes suggests that 'rough outs' were transported from the 'factory' and then polished and finished locally. Both the rock and the axes may therefore have had some special significance or status (By permission of the National Museum of Wales).

THE FIRST FARMERS

There followed a revolutionary change in human behaviour. This was the advent of farming - the systematic control of the land to produce regular supplies of food - which was introduced to Wales about 4,000 B.C. by emigrants from the now sea-separated continent of Europe.

Clearing the forested land for crops or pasture required the use of axes with heads of good quality stone. These were often traded over remarkably long distances, and axes from the 'factory' at Graig Lwyd, Conwy, have been found as far afield as Yorkshire. Evidence from other sites, moreover, indicates that axe heads were deliberately quarried from dangerous and scarcely accessible cliff-faces, even though the stone there was of no better quality than elsewhere in the area. These factors suggest that axes from particular places had some special significance beyond their usefulness as tools, and it is even possible that they were among the earliest symbols of power and status.

St Lythan's chambered tomb (Vale of Glamorgan), now denuded of its covering mound. It is clear from the massive surviving stones that a very considerable group effort would have been required to erect this monument.

THE GREAT COMMUNAL TOMBS

Far more obvious symbols of power - of a sort - are the great communal tombs raised by the New Stone Age farmers on their newly-cleared territories. Constructed of massive stones ('megaliths'), a millennium before the earliest Egyptian pyramids, these monuments required very considerable group effort and organization. More than two hundred people, for instance, must have been needed to position the huge fifty ton capstone - the largest in mainland Britain - at Tinkinswood in the Vale of Glamorgan. Originally covered by mounds of earth or stone (since often eroded away), many tombs were also equipped with 'courtyards' in front of their entrances, doubtless used for communal rituals to honour the dead. Indeed, it is clear that they were not merely burial places, but also shrines to the ancestors, the focus of the community, and the proclamation of its power in the land.

These great houses of the dead were in use over long periods, sometimes as much as a thousand years. Within them were placed the disjointed bones of generations of men, women and children, anonymously jumbled together, and without grave goods or other means of individual identification. Who these people were is unknown, though it seems likely that they belonged to a group with special status, perhaps as the direct descendants of the earliest settlers. Their individual anonymity, however, implies that the tombs celebrated the triumph of the continuing community over transitory human lives, and perhaps of communal over personal power.

The same might be said of the new types of monument which appear about a thousand years after the coming of the first farmers - stone circles and alignments. Whether these were meeting places, religious centres or even astronomical observatories - or all, or none of these things - it seems all but certain that they were raised by and for whole communities. By about 2,500 B.C., however, symbols of individual power and status were being created in Wales.

Right: Penrhos Feilw standing stones on Holyhead Island, Anglesey. Whatever their purpose, such monuments were almost certainly erected by, and for, communal groups.

AN AGE OF CHIEFTAINS

rom about 2,500 B.C. onwards, burial
aditions changed from communal to
dividual graves, with the body
ccompanied by elaborate grave goods.
his development marked a move
wards greater emphasis upon the
dividual, in place of the communal
lentity evident in the earlier tradition.
n this reconstruction of a cist burial
om Brymbo, Wrexham, (*above*) the
keleton of a man is accompanied by
'beaker' and flint flake knife.
Beakers' were often elaborately
ecorated like the example from
lanharry, near Llantrisant (*right*), and
ere perhaps prized items of status (By
ermission of the National Museum of Wales).

BARROWS AND BEAKERS

The last two and a half millennia of the prehistoric period were times of marked and cumulative change, as the emphasis shifted from communal to personal power, and progressively more competitive societies came to be dominated by tribal chieftains and warrior aristocracies. The earliest harbingers of change - appearing from about 2,500 B.C. onwards - were individual burials beneath mounded 'round barrows', often accompanied by decorated pottery 'beakers' and personal weapons. Thus the people commemorated clearly saw themselves as distinct personalities, as opposed to anonymous members of a community. They may have been entrepreneurial immigrants from Europe, or natives under the influence of a new belief system which emphasized individual status, warfare - and drinking, for some beakers originally contained a mead-like alcohol flavoured with herbs or fruit. At first apparently 'outsiders' (whose burial-mounds avoided older religious centres) they eventually became a ruling class. Their dramatically-sited barrows even now dominate many a Welsh skyline, staking a visual claim to the surrounding territory.

about **2,500 B.C.**	More land cleared. Individual burials replace communal tombs. Round barrows built.
about **2000 B.C.**	Bronze Age. Uplands deforested. Widespread metalworking. Society becoming more hierarchical.
about **700 - 600 B.C.**	Early Iron Age. Wales increasingly under Celtic influence. Widespread construction of hillforts.
about **200 B.C. - A.D.100**	Wales divided into recognizable tribal territories.
A.D. 48	First Roman attacks on Wales.

Below: One of a number of arrow heads from the so-called 'archer's grave' at Breach Farm, Llanblethian, Vale of Glamorgan (By permission of the National Museum of Wales).

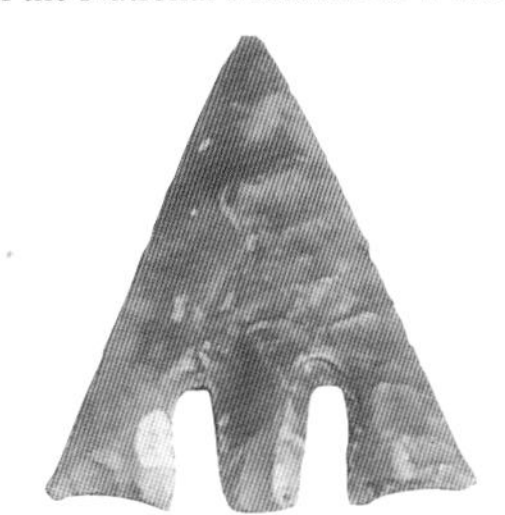

Left: Round barrows were frequently sited in prominent locations, like these three cairns surrounded by the later Iron Age hillfort at Foel Trigarn, Pembrokeshire (By courtesy of The Royal Commisssion on the Ancient and Historical Monuments of Wales).

Left: The superb gold 'lunula' from Llanllynfi, Gwynedd. A cord or chain was probably fastened to the terminals so that the ornament could be worn suspended over the chest of the proud owner. Similar objects found elsewhere in Europe are recognized as the badges of warrior aristocrats (By permission of the National Museum of Wales).

Below: A cape of beaten gold from Mold, Flintshire. This magnificent object was found enclosing part of a skeleton in a cist burial covered by a cairn; with it were over three hundred amber beads and the remains of coarse cloth. This ostentatious disposal of wealth in a grave must mark the burial of a person of some special status (By kind permission of the Trustees of the British Museum).

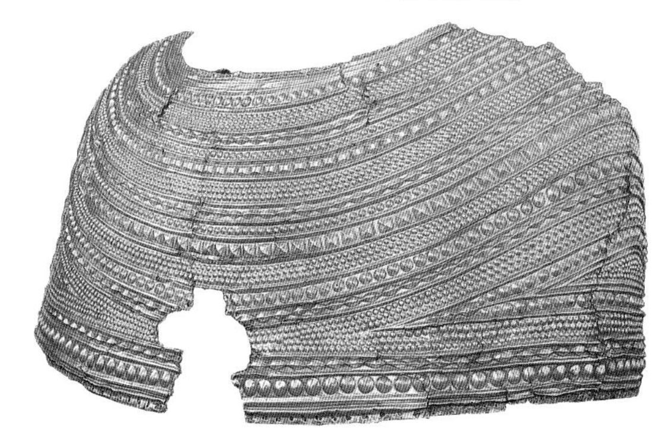

BRONZE AND GOLD

Later 'round barrows' also contain new status symbols: daggers, axes and other bronze weapons, products of the metal-working technology well established in Wales by 2000 B.C. Still more potent symbols of power were splendid gold ornaments, available only to the wealthy leaders of an increasingly hierarchical society. The amazing gold 'cape' discovered in a burial mound at Mold, Flintshire, must surely have adorned a Bronze Age chieftain, as must the moon-shaped 'lunula' from Llanllyfni and the golden bracelets and 'torcs' - or neck rings - recognized throughout late prehistoric Europe as the badges of warrior aristocrats - found elsewhere in Wales.

The tendency towards a warlike, chieftain-dominated society was dramatically accelerated by the catastrophic climate deterioration which occurred around 1400-1200 B.C. In Wales, the onset of much colder weather triggered a man-made ecological disaster, as the easily-deforested but quickly exhausted uplands became the infertile wildernesses they have remained ever since. Amid

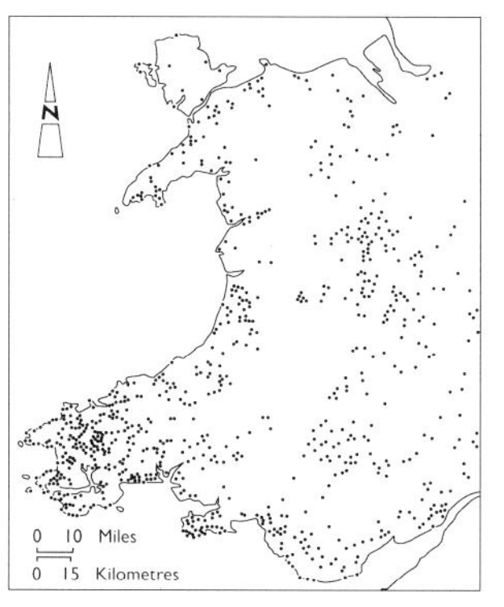

Map of Iron Age Hillforts in Wales and the Borders

he resulting competition for the remaining armland, new types of weapons developed, and ommunities began for the first time to defend their ettlements with fortifications of earth and stone.

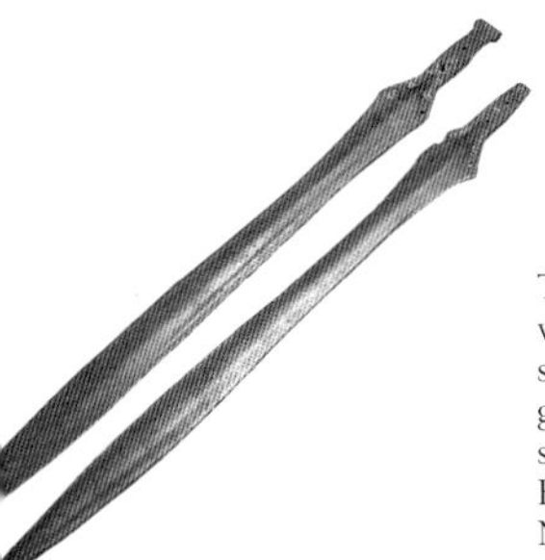

The increased appearance of weapons such as these bronze swords seems to indicate the growth of a more warlike society from about 1400-1200 B.C. (By permission of the National Museum of Wales).

HILLFORTS

ome six hundred such 'hillforts' - a fifth of the ritish total - survive in Wales. The great majority vere raised during the 'Iron Age', the period from bout 600 B.C. onwards, when tools and weapons f iron increasingly superseded those of bronze. Velsh hillforts vary widely in size, type and omplexity, but nearly all exploit the natural trength of hilltop or - on the western and southern oasts - cliff-edge sites.

In mountainous areas their ramparts (as at Foel rigarn, Pembrokeshire, or Tre'r Ceiri, Gwynedd) night be constructed of dry-stone walling, but more ften they were defended by single or multiple ystems of ditches and earthen banks, reinforced in tone, and originally topped by timber stockades. here are also clear distinctions of strength and tatus. The small, simple forts of south-west Wales vere probably no more than lightly-defended armsteads, while the great multi-ramparted forts f the eastern borders were the power-centres of nportant tribal chieftains, dominating clearly-efined territories and ruling populations numbered n thousands.

By the early first century A.D., indeed, the land vas divided between recognizable tribal groups: the ilures in the south-east; the Cornovii in the central orders; the Deceangli in the north-east; the)rdovices in the north-west, and the Demetae in the outh-west. Their names were set down by the owerful invaders who ushered Wales from rehistory into recorded history - the Romans.

eft: Pen y Crug Iron Age hillfort, Powys. Between four and five amparts and ditches skirt the contours to exploit the maximum efensive strength of the hilltop position. No doubt the site would lso have served as a powerful symbol of tribal control, dominating he local terrain for many miles around (By courtesy of The Royal ommission on the Ancient and Historical Monuments of Wales).

IRON AGE CHIEFTAINS

The dry-stone built ramparts of the Iron Age hillfort of Tre'r Ceiri, Gwynedd (By courtesy of The Royal Commission on the Ancient and Historical Monuments of Wales).

Dominating a society which pre-dated written records, the chieftains of Iron Age Wales are necessarily anonymous. Yet the essence of their flamboyant lifestyle can be gleaned from Classical descriptions of their European contemporaries, backed up by archaeological finds from Wales itself. Many of these come from pools or bogs, wherein they were cast as sacrifices to water deities.

Roman writers called the Celts 'war-mad and quick to battle', and the most important chiefly power symbols were undoubtedly weapons, notably spears and swords. Swords were generally bronze, though prestigious iron swords like a fragment known from Llyn Fawr were later imported from Europe.

Chieftains were expected to feast their warbands royally, and banquets were occasions when heroic deeds were proclaimed or disputed. A wrought-iron firedog from Capel Garmon supported a spit for roasting meat. It is appropriately decorated with the heads of cattle, and extensive herds were an important attribute of aristocratic status.

Horses were also used in warfare, and their high status is demonstrated by their elaborate trappings. Reflecting the recorded Celtic love of decoration, a bronze plaque from Llyn Cerrig Bach, Anglesey, may have adorned a war-chariot.

Raiders also carried off captives as slaves, and chiefly society maintained rigid distinctions between free warriors and servile workers. Two iron gang-chains from Llyn Cerrig Bach recall its darker aspects.

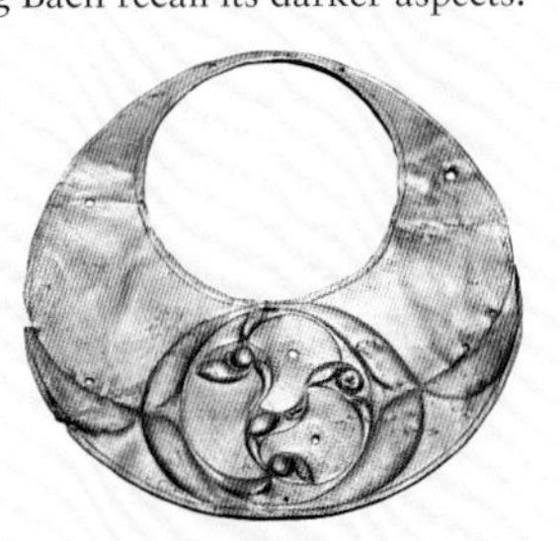

Above: *The ornately embossed bronze plaque from the Llyn Cerrig Bach hoard, Anglesey (By permission of the National Museum of Wales).*

Above: *The wrought-iron firedog from Capel Garmon, Clwyd (By permission of the National Museum of Wales).*

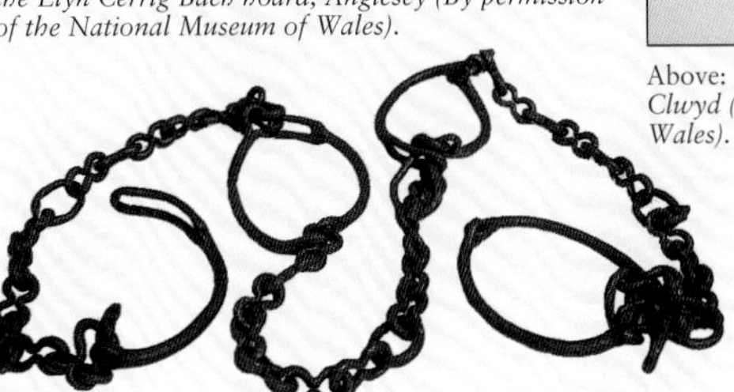

Left: *One of the two iron gang-chains from the Llyn Cerrig Bach hoard, Anglesey (By permission of the National Museum of Wales).*

THE IMPACT OF ROME

A.D. 48 - 80	Roman military conquest of Wales. Forts and roads built.
A.D. 120 - 300	Internal peace and prosperity as Wales assimilated into Roman Empire. Chieftains become Romano-British citizens.
A.D. 275 - 380	Increasing threat from Irish raiders: coastal defences built.
A.D. 400	Direct Roman rule peters out: beginning of Romano-Welsh princedoms.

THE ROMAN CONQUEST: SOLDIERS, FORTS AND ROADS

The Romans invaded Britain in A.D. 43, subduing what is now southern England within five years. They found the conquest of Wales a far more difficult task, requiring more than three decades of intermittent fighting. Thirteen separate campaigns, involving up to 30,000 Roman soldiers, were needed before stubborn guerrilla resistance was finally overcome by about A.D. 75-80.

During the earlier stages of Roman rule, there could be no doubt that the formidably efficient Roman army exercised power in the land, and no mistaking the instrument and symbol of its domination - the highly organized system of Roman forts and roads. Forts were constructed by the soldiers themselves. Expeditionary forces entrenched their temporary 'marching camps' against surprise attack, and permanent forts were subsequently built to garrison conquered territory. The largest were legionary fortresses, long-term bases for around 5,500 elite infantry. Four were established during the conquest of Wales - at *Burrium* (Usk) in Monmouthshire, *Deva* (Chester), *Viroconium* (Wroxeter, Shropshire) and *Isca* - Caerleon, near Newport, headquarters of the Second Augustan Legion between A.D. 75 and about A.D. 290.

In addition, a network of some thirty-five lesser forts held down Wales and the borders, each garrisoned by a force of auxiliary infantry or cavalry. For mutual support, these forts were built at intervals of a day's march - some 12 miles (20km) apart. Thus the metalled roads which linked them were as vital an instrument of Roman rule as the forts themselves: long-lasting symbols of power, many remained in use throughout the Middle Ages, and some are even now followed by modern routeways.

Originally built in earth and timber, most forts were later provided with stone walls and gateways. By A.D. 200, however, very few were still fully garrisoned. No longer conquerors and conquered, 'Romans' and 'Britons' were becoming one people.

FROM CHIEFTAINS TO CITIZENS

This process of assimilation was to have long-term effects on the development of Wales as a separate entity. It began soon after the campaigns of conquest ended, when as a matter of policy the former native 'ruling class' was encouraged to adopt Roman ways and town-based civilization. Settlements grew up around forts like Caerleon and *Segontium* (Caernarfon), and new self-governing towns were deliberately founded at Carmarthen and Caerwent.

Segontium (Caernarfon) · Chester · Wroxeter · Brecon · Carmarthen · Neath · Usk · Caerleon · Sea Mills · DECEANGLI · ORDOVICES · DEMETAE · SILURES · N · 0 10 Miles · 0 15 Kilometres

Roman Forts in Wales and the Marches

- ■ Legionary Fortress
- □ Legionary Fortress (evacuated)
- ▪ Fort
- ▫ Fortlet
- ⋯ Roads

Right: A reconstruction of the *forum-basilica*, the centre of public life, within the deliberately founded Roman town of Caerwent. The complex - a Rome in miniature - was soon adopted as a symbol of status by the native Romano-Britons (Illustration by John Banbury).

Above: A bronze plaque depicting a winged victory with a trophy over her shoulder, from the Prysg Field barracks, Caerleon. It is possibly a fragment of parade armour, or perhaps decoration for a portable shrine. The image, however, captures the formidable might of the Roman Imperial army (By permission of the National Museum of Wales).

Left: The Prysg Field barrack blocks at the Roman legionary fortress of Caerleon. The fortress occupied a key position in the highly organized system of Roman forts in Wales - a system that was both the instrument and symbol of the domination of the Roman army (Photograph by Skyscan).

The surviving inscribed statue base set up by the council of the Silures to honour the legionary commander, Tiberius Claudius Paulinus, at Caerwent. Such acts of tribute by the tribal council indicate both the civilian power held by the native inhabitants and the degree to which they had become Romanized.

Known as *Venta Silurum*, 'the market town of the Silures', Caerwent became the 'tribal capital' of that once-hostile people. Silurian chieftains, persuaded to abandon their hillforts, became its first town councillors. A Rome in miniature, it boasted a *forum-basilica* or 'town hall', as well as parades of shops and town houses - new symbols of status for Romano-Britons. By A.D. 220, when the 'Silurian republic' erected a statue to an honoured legionary commander, all upper-class Britons had been officially decreed Roman citizens.

Elsewhere in Wales - especially the north and west - Romanization made less progress, and chieftains kept to their hillforts and fortified farms. But when external forces began to threaten Wales towards the end of the third century A.D., little formal distinction can have remained between 'Roman' and 'native'.

THE END AND THE BEGINNING

This threat emanated from sea-borne Irish raids, and to counter them new coastal defences - reminders of still-formidable Imperial power - were raised at Cardiff and elsewhere, while new turrets strengthened the walls of Caerwent and the garrison of *Segontium* was reinforced. Roman regular forces in Wales, however, were increasingly called away to crises elsewhere in the empire, or to further the ambitions of generals. The most important of these was Magnus Maximus, who withdrew troops from Britain to help him become emperor in A.D. 383: they never returned, and Maximus was blamed for exposing the land to barbarian invaders.

Yet to later Welsh tradition Maximus was a hero, hailed as the founder of princely dynasties. Seemingly he encouraged the citizen-nobility of Roman Wales to organize their own defence, setting them on the road to independence. When direct Roman rule petered out after about A.D. 400, it was certainly they who filled the vacuum of power. During the obscure centuries which saw the beginnings of Wales as a distinct nation, their descendants would emerge as its first princes.

A coin of the emperor Magnus Maximus. Coinage was an important symbol of Imperial power Maximus, too, later became a symbol for the rise of a distinct Welsh nation, and was hailed as the founder of princely dynasties (By permission of the National Museum of Wales).

Right: The south wall of the Roman town of Caerwent. The towers were added to the existing town wall in the mid fourth century as an additional defensive measure against the threat of invading barbarians. Similar protective action was taken at a number of locations in Wales, including Cardiff.

THE BEGINNING OF WALES

he history of the emergence of Wales as a nation in the post-.oman period is clouded by legend - the so-called 'Matter of ritain'. This manuscript illustration shows one such episode in /hich Vortigern, terrified by the fighting dragons - the red ymbolizing the Britons and the white the Saxons - relinquished his :own and fortress to Ambrosius or Emrys. The site of this onfrontation is traditionally held to be Dinas Emrys in Snowdonia 3y courtesy of Lambeth Palace Library, Ms. 6, f. 43v).

The period between A.D. 400 and 800 is perhaps the most important in the history of Wales,)ecause it witnessed the birth of the nation. At its)utset, Wales was part of the Roman empire, ;overned at least nominally by Imperial officials:)efore its end, Wales was a distinct entity, divided)etween independent native rulers.

These crucial centuries, however, are also the :ast understood period of Welsh history. Their)bscurity is further clouded by legends about figures ike Vortigern, Merlin and, above all, King Arthur. The influence of such quasi-historical tales is eflected in the names given to monuments all over Wales. The circular Roman amphitheatre at :aerleon, for example, was long known as 'King Arthur's Round Table', while 'Arthur's Stone' in Gower - probably the capstone of a prehistoric tomb was allegedly a pebble from his shoe.

THE HEIRS OF ROME

What seems certain is that the earliest independent Welsh rulers regarded themselves as the heirs of Rome. For at least a century after A.D. 400, they continued to use Roman titles like 'protector', 'magistrate' and 'citizen': 'prince' and 'king' came later, signalling a growing confidence in a new tradition of native power. Yet as late as A.D. 850, Eliseg's Pillar (near Llangollen, Denbighshire) still proudly proclaimed the descent of the princes of Powys from 'Maximus, King of the Romans'.

They were also the inheritors of an older tradition of power, that of the Iron Age chieftains who ruled before Rome came. The collapse of Roman town-based civilisation, indeed, resulted in a widespread revival of the ancient hillfort power centres. The rock of Degannwy, Conwy, for instance, was traditionally the stronghold of Maelgwyn Gwynedd (d. 547), first recorded king of north-west Wales. Such princely strongholds were praised by the bards who accompanied every prince's retinue, and whose task was to enhance their patron's prestige by publicizing his lineage, his generosity, and his victories over rival rulers.

Right: Eliseg's Pillar, near Llangollen, Denbighshire. The inscription records the ancestry and ancient glories of the kings of Powys right back to 'Maximus, King of the Romans'.
Below: The defended hilltop site of Dinas Emrys, Gwynedd - the legendary site of Vortigern's capitulation to Ambrosius or Emrys, a symbolic triumph of the Britons over the Saxon invaders.

about **A.D. 450**	First Early Christian Monuments erected.
about **A.D. 540**	Earliest record of Welsh princes.
about **A.D. 600 - 800**	Many small Welsh kingdoms.
about **A.D. 640**	Anglo-Saxon threat increases.
about **A.D. 784 - 96**	Offa's Dyke built.
about **A.D. 800**	Fewer and larger Welsh kingdoms. Appearance of free-standing crosses.
about **A.D. 870 - 950**	Periods of unity under Rhodri the Great and Hywel the Good.
about **1057 - 63**	Wales united by Gruffudd ap Llywelyn.

Carew Cross, Pembrokeshire, erected in memory of Maredudd ab Edwin who became ruler of Deheubarth (the kingdom of south-west Wales) in 1033. Some 450 Early Christian memorial stones survive from the period between about A.D. 450 and 1100, many of which record the titles and ancestry of those they commemorate, thus serving as symbols of power as well as of faith.

THE CHRISTIAN CYMRY

Despite their internecine feuds, the many independent rulers of post-Roman Wales gradually came to see themselves as 'Cymry' - 'fellow countrymen'. Among the factors which united them were their common Welsh language and their Christian religion, established in later Roman times and proclaimed on the gravestones of princes, nobles and churchmen which are by far the most frequently-surviving monuments of the period. Some 450 remain, ranging in date from the fifth to the eleventh century and in elaboration from roughly-cut inscriptions to beautifully sculpted 'high crosses' like those at Carew and Nevern. Many record the titles and ancestry of those they commemorate, serving as symbols of power as well as of faith.

THE ANGLO-SAXON THREAT

Probably the most important unifying factor, however, was the threat posed by the Anglo-Saxons, the originally pagan 'English' whose armies had reached the natural boundaries of Wales - the rivers Wye, Severn and Dee - by the mid-600s. Their slaughter of Cynddylan, the last Welsh prince to rule what is now the Shrewsbury area, was long remembered with anguish by his fellow countrymen.

Cynddylan's hall is dark tonight,
Without fire, without candle.
But for God, who will give me sanity?

A century of border wars later, the mighty Anglo-Saxon king, Offa of Mercia, raised the most impressive of all symbols of power in early medieval Britain - Offa's Dyke.

Above: A penny showing the head and inscription of Offa - *Offa Rex* - the mighty Anglo-Saxon king of Mercia (By kind permission of the Trustees of the British Museum).

Probably constructed between A.D. 784 and 796 to define a frontier stretching from the Irish Sea to the Bristol Channel, this tremendous earthwork extends intermittently for over 80 miles (128km). Its ditched rampart, still stands up to 25 feet (8m) high, and in places runs in straight alignments for over 12 miles (20km) - evidence of skilled engineering as well as a massive organized labour force. A boundary marker rather than a fortification, the dyke brought no end to border wars. Yet it retains its immense symbolic importance to this day. For it unmistakably separated Anglo-Saxon England from the now distinct nation of Wales - the Kingdoms of the Cymry.

A section of Offa's Dyke, near Chirk Castle. Built in the latter half of the eighth century, it was the longest as well as the most striking man-made boundary in medieval western Europe, and played an important role in shaping the perception of the extent and identity of Wales (By courtesy of The Royal Commission on Ancient and Historical Monuments in Wales).

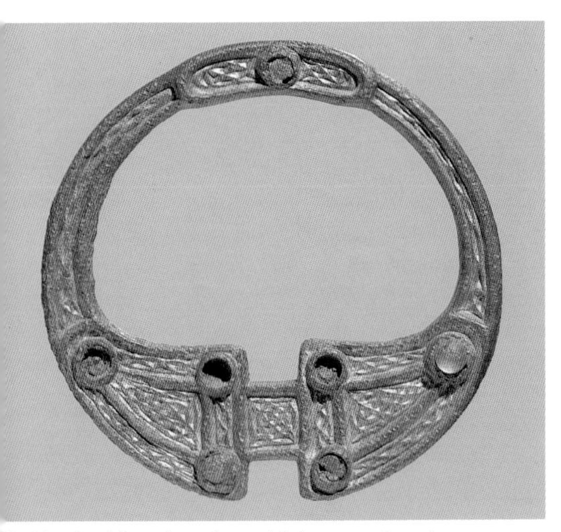

'he Llys Awel Farm brooch: an eighth-century 'pseudo-enannular' brooch, richly decorated with gilt, glass beads and mber studs. The skills of craftsmen were highly regarded and such ne jewellery was probably a much-prized possession of a wealthy lite (By permission of the National Museum of Wales).

KINGDOMS OF THE CYMRY

Between the building of Offa's Dyke and the Norman invasions, the many small princedoms of post-Roman Wales increasingly coalesced into larger realms, dominated by a few powerful dynasties - most notably the rulers of Gwynedd, descendants of Maximus and Maelgwyn of Degannwy. Outstanding princes of this house strove towards national unity, and Rhodri the Great reigned over nearly three-quarters of Wales before his death at English hands in A.D. 877. His grandson Hywel Dda - Hywel the Good - ruled more widely still. Again his empire disintegrated after his death in about A.D. 950, yet an enduring symbol of his power survived in the Welsh laws he codified for the nation, some of which remained in force until the Acts of Union of 1536/43.

Only once, however, did Wales briefly become a single unit. In 1057, Gruffudd ap Llywelyn of Gwynedd completed a bloodstained rise to power, becoming the only native prince ever to rule the whole land. But seven years later he too was overthrown by an English invasion, leaving the Welsh princes divided in the face of the imminent Norman onslaught.

Right: A Welsh prince as a lawgiver, from a mid-thirteenth-century copy of the great Welsh law book of Hywel Dda - Hywel the Good (By courtesy of the National Library of Wales, Peniarth Ms. 28, f. 1v).

COURTS OF THE PRINCES

The Llangorse 'crannog', seen here during excavation, was probably built for the kings of Brycheiniog in about A.D. 900 (By courtesy of The Royal Commission on Ancient and Historical Monuments in Wales).

Excavation at two Welsh sites has revealed much about the residences of early medieval princes, and the trappings of power which surrounded them. The first is Dinas Powys near Cardiff, where a hilltop was fortified with multiple banks and ditches in the late fifth century, and occupied until the seventh. Rich finds there demonstrate that its owners were neither barbarous nor isolated from the outside world.

They and their retinues drank Mediterranean wine, and imported glass, metalwork and pottery from France and the Anglo-Saxon lands, while skilled court craftsmen worked at hearths on the site to produce jewellery of bronze and gold. Clearly the lords of Dinas Powys were men of high status, perhaps rulers of the local princedom of Glywysing.

An even more remarkable discovery - still being investigated - is the royal 'crannog' (or artificial island) set in Llangorse Lake near Brecon, Powys. Ingeniously constructed of brushwood and boulders, reinforced and stockaded in timber, such man-made island strongholds were previously unknown in Wales or England, though familiar in Scotland and Ireland. The Llangorse crannog, indeed, was probably built in about A.D. 900 for the kings of Brycheiniog, who boasted descent from an immigrant Irish chieftain. Apart from rare finds of high-quality cloth - perhaps fragments of embroidered hangings or princely garments - the site has also produced metalworking evidence, including an Irish style brooch and part of a container for holy relics. It also bears the marks of its destruction in A.D. 916, when an English raiding force carried off the wife of King Tewdwr ap Elised and thirty-three of his courtiers.

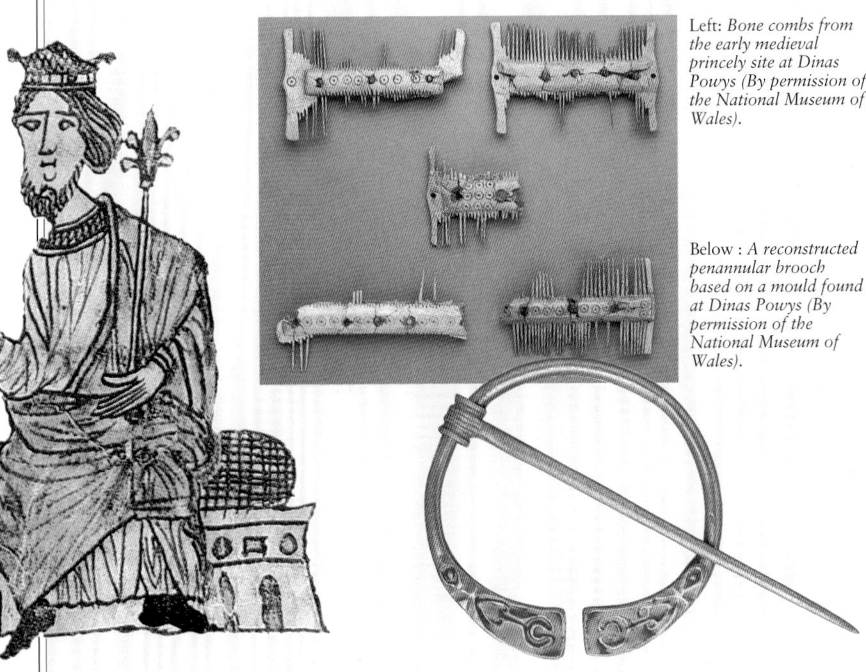

Left: *Bone combs from the early medieval princely site at Dinas Powys (By permission of the National Museum of Wales).*

Below : *A reconstructed penannular brooch based on a mould found at Dinas Powys (By permission of the National Museum of Wales).*

THE NORMAN ONSLAUGHT

The stone shell keep atop the earthen 'motte' or mound at Cardiff Castle. Castles rapidly became the Norman symbol of power as well as the instrument of conquest. Often they were first built as earthen 'motte and bailey' constructions and later strengthened by stone fortifications.

During the later eleventh and twelfth centuries, the power structure of Wales was transformed by the Normans. Unlike their rapid seizure of England under William the Conqueror, the Norman assault on Wales was a long-drawn-out, piecemeal affair, principally the work of freebooting barons and knights known as 'Marchers' - 'borderers' or 'frontiersmen'. Their title to power was in no way legal or hereditary, being based entirely on military force: as The Domesday Book recorded of the Marcher knight Osbern fitz Richard, 'he has what he can take, nothing more'. Its instruments and symbols were two formidable new weapons: the knight and the castle.

KNIGHTS AND CASTLES

Mailclad Norman knights were the most feared warriors in Europe. Highly trained, expensively equipped, and mounted on specially bred warhorses, they were reckoned unbeatable in open country. But they were rather less effective amid the mountains and woods of Wales, where they needed castles as fortified campaign bases. Some of the earliest were built by the powerful noblemen (like William fitz Osbern, earl of Hereford) whose territories formed a buffer-zone along the English border, and who used castles like fitz Osbern's Chepstow and Monmouth as springboards for expansion into Wales itself.

The onslaught was continued by free-enterprise land-grabbing expeditions, fighting their way along coasts and river valleys and raising earth and timber castles as they went. These easily constructed fortresses were focused on a stockade-topped mound (or 'motte') strong-point, below which extended a defended enclosure (or 'bailey') to protect horses and living quarters. Wiston Castle in Pembrokeshire is a fine example of such simple 'motte and bailey' castles, which were far more numerous and closely-set in Wales than in any other part of Britain. Though some were soon abandoned as the tide of conquest advanced, others - like Ogmore in the Vale of Glamorgan - were strengthened in stone to consolidate the Norman hold on occupied areas. Frequently updated and enlarged, castles like this would remain the dominant symbols of power in Wales for over four centuries.

Norman knights, clad in mail and mounted on specially bred warhorses, were a formidable fighting force, as shown in this scene from the Bayeux tapestry.

THE FRAGMENTATION OF POWER

The large number of developed castles in Wales reflects the fragmentation of power produced by two centuries of shifting boundaries and intermittent, often localized warfare. At first, Norman attacks were disastrously successful, so that it seemed they might overrun the whole land. Then came a series of Welsh counter-attacks, and by 1105 an uneasy equipoise had been established, with the marchers generally dominating the eastern borders and southern lowlands, while the Welsh princes held the uplands and the north and west.

Nor was this the limit of fragmentation. For the Welsh-held lands were divided between the major princedoms of Gwynedd, Deheubarth and Powys and several smaller realms, while the Norman 'Marches' were a jigsaw of independent 'lordships' ruled by the successors of the adventurers who had first seized them. Individual Marchers and princes, moreover, might attempt to expand their own holdings at the expense of their fellow-countrymen, sometimes by allying with 'enemy' rulers.

MARCHERS AND PRINCES

The balance of power in this fragmented land turned partly on occasional interventions by the kings of England, but far more upon the emergence of outstandingly able or ruthless leaders. Thus the first Norman earl of Chester - Hugh of Avranches, alias 'Hugh the Fat' (d. 1101) - penetrated deep into north Wales and almost conquered Gwynedd: but his

about **1070**	First Norman attacks on Wales. First castles in Wales.
about **1090 - 95**	High tide of Norman onslaught.
about **1105**	Welsh counter-attacks stem invasion. Approximate boundaries between Welsh and Norman lands established.
about **1175**	The Lord Rhys dominant in south Wales.
about **1200**	Llywelyn the Great succeeds to Gwynedd.

Above: A silver penny of Henry I (1100-35) minted at Cardiff. The presence of a mint at Cardiff suggests that it was a securely held site of some importance at this time (By permission of the National Museum of Wales).

Left: The Great Tower at Chepstow, occupies part of the first castle built by William Fitz Osbern.

WILLIAM MARSHAL

Above: *The handsome tomb effigy of William Marshal in the Temple Church, City of London.*

William Marshal (about 1146-1219) was highly unusual in achieving power through his unswerving loyalty and unblemished honour: his rise from landless esquire to Regent of England, recorded in a near-contemporary biography, reads like a chivalric romance. The younger son of a modest family, his knightly reputation was founded on his prowess in tournaments and maintained by his fidelity to four successive Plantagenet monarchs - Henry II, Richard I, John and Henry III - steadfastly maintained throughout their bitter family feuds.

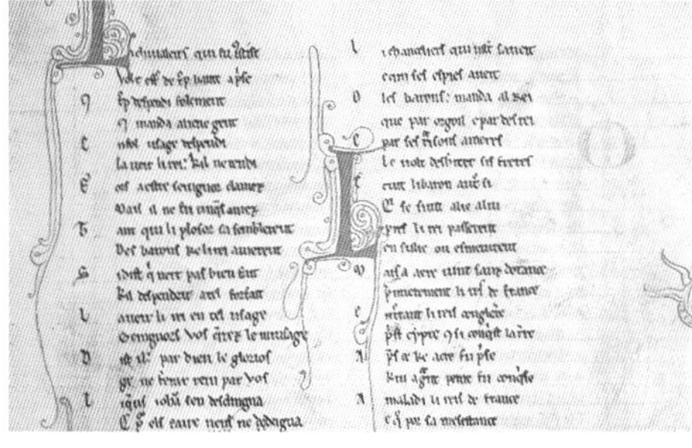

A section from the near-contemporary biography of William Marshal - 'L'Histoire de Guillaume le Mareschal' *(By courtesy of the Morgan Library, New York).*

Unusually, too, the foundation of Marshal's power in Wales was marriage, not conquest. In 1189 Henry II rewarded him with the heiress of wide lands in south Wales, England, Ireland and France, and nine years later he was confirmed as earl of Pembroke and Chepstow. At both these places he raised castles notable for their technical innovations - the twin-towered gatehouse and round-towered curtain walls at Chepstow, and the great round keep (the earliest in Wales) at Pembroke. A major influence in Welsh politics, he strove - not always successfully - to contain the growing power of Llywelyn the Great.

In 1216, though over seventy years old, William was unanimously chosen as regent for the infant King Henry III. He died universally respected in 1219, and was buried in the church of the Templar Knights (for whom he had fought in the Holy Land) in London. His surviving effigy there, portrays him in his knightly panoply, mailclad and bearing a shield emblazoned with his heraldic arms. Such heraldry, also used on the seals which confirmed legal transactions, was by now becoming firmly established as a symbol of individual power and nobility, instantly identifiable in a largely illiterate age.

Below: *An early fourteenth-century manuscript illustration depicting the coronation of King Richard I. William 'the Marshal', participated in the ceremony by carrying the gold sceptre with the cross (By permission of the British Library, Royal Ms. 16 G VI f. 347V).*

This fourteenth-century tomb effigy in St Davids Cathedral is reputedly that of Rhys ap Gruffudd - 'The Lord Rhys' - who successfully ruled much of south Wales in the mid to late twelfth century.

designs were balked by Gruffudd ap Cynan (about 1055-1137), the half-Welsh, half-Viking hero of the earliest Welsh biography. Two generations later, the great Rhys ap Gruffudd - 'The Lord Rhys' (d. 1197) - repelled the Norman assault on Deheubarth, winning recognition from King Henry II of England as the effective ruler of all south Wales. But his last years were clouded by the counter-attacks of the unscrupulous William de Braose (d. 1211), who exploited his friendship with King John to swallow up the lands of Marchers and princes alike.

The power of such men depended not only on skill in warfare, but also on personal diplomacy and the adroit manipulation of family marriage alliances with neighbours of either race. The multiple romances of the beautiful Welsh Princess Nest, indeed, produced a remarkable brood of 'Norman-Welshmen'. They included the leaders of the Norman-Welsh invasion of Ireland - which adopted the warcry 'St David' - and the famous, multi-talented Giraldus Cambrensis, 'Gerald of Wales'. By turns scholar, author, courtier of English kings and champion of the Welsh Church, Gerald's blend of Norman and Welsh blood gave him unique insights into the divided land that bred him. The remedy for its ills, he wrote, was either final conquest by the kings of England or a national alliance of all Welshmen behind a single native ruler. When Gerald died in 1223, it was the latter solution that seemed likeliest to be realized.

Left: The great round keep at Pembroke Castle built by William Marshal soon after 1200-01. It is thought to be the inspiration for both Marcher and Welsh round towers. In turn, Pembroke itself was inspired by the round towers put up in northern France by King Philip Augustus (1180-1223) in the late twelfth century.

THE AGE OF THE LLYWELYNS

The thirteenth century saw Wales moving closer to unified nationhood, as power became oncentrated into the hands of outstanding princes f Gwynedd: after rolling back the boundaries of the Aarches, they briefly achieved recognition of their tatus from the kings of England. The first was lywelyn ab Iorwerth (Llywelyn the Great).

lywelyn ab Iorwerth - the Great, as the premier Welsh prince, nerited a castle to match those raised by his allies and adversaries. lere, at Dolbadarn Castle, he constructed a massive round tower vhich incorporated the latest advances in military technology.

THE MARCHER REACTION

The seemingly inexorable growth of Llywelyn's power rang alarm bells among the Marchers. They reacted by building stronger fortresses, which often featured the new-style round keeps and wall-towers pioneered by William Marshal at Pembroke and Chepstow, and built by his sons at Cilgerran. Round keeps rose at Bronllys and Tretower in the Brecon region and at Skenfrith in Monmouthshire - areas newly threatened by resurgent Welsh power - while a

1218 - 1240	Llywelyn the Great dominates Wales.
1258	Llywelyn ap Gruffudd receives oaths of homage and allegiance from Welsh princes.
1267	Llywelyn acknowledged as 'Prince of Wales' and rules three-quarters of Wales; threatens remaining Marcher territory.
1277	Edward I invades Gwynedd.

powerful royal border fortress was established at Montgomery. Only Llywelyn's death in 1240, however, called a temporary halt to Welsh advances: but by then he had demonstrated beyond doubt that a single strong prince was the best hope for the Welsh nation.

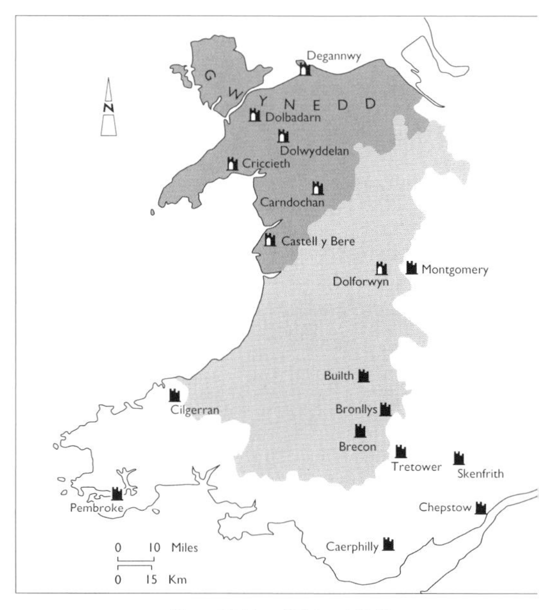

Map of Wales: 1234 and 1267

Welsh Castles

English Castles

Territories of Llywelyn ab Iorwerth 1234

Extent of territories subject to Llywelyn ap Gruffudd 1267

LLYWELYN THE GREAT

Llywelyn ab Iorwerth, who descended from the earliest princes of north Wales, succeeded to Gwynedd in 1200. By 1218 he was acknowledged as effective ruler of native Wales both by his fellow countrymen and by a weakened English government. Honoured as 'Llywelyn the Great', he strove to create the foundations of a unified monarchy by becoming not merely the leader, but also the legal overlord of all other Welsh rulers. As a symbol of this new and special status, he alone used the title of 'prince'.

Married to the illegitimate daughter of King John of England, Llywelyn adapted the trappings of English royal power to his own purpose. Thus he created a vestigial 'civil service' and used Great and Private Seals to validate princely grants.

The castles he built to defend his expanding realm also display a blend of native and modernizing elements. His earlier fortresses - like Castell y Bere and Castell Carndochan - have characteristically Welsh D-shaped keep-towers: yet Castell y Bere also boasts fine stone carving in the latest international style. His later strongholds, moreover, incorporate the most up-to-date military technology, like Criccieth's twin-towered gatehouse and Dolbadarn's mighty round keep.

Above: *This stone carved image was found at Llywelyn's castle at Degannwy and may be a contemporary representation of the prince (By permission of the National Museum of Wales).*

Left: *The privy, or private, seal of Llywelyn ab Iorwerth - Llywelyn the Great (By permission of the National Museum of Wales).*

Below: *Finely carved stonework has been recovered from another of Llywelyn's castles, at Castell y Bere, demonstrating the Welsh prince's concern with a conspicuous display of status (By permission of the National Museum of Wales).*

Below: *Llywelyn's formidable twin-towered gatehouse at Criccieth Castle: it incorporated the most up-to-date military technology and was probably inspired by contemporary work at Beeston Castle, Cheshire.*

THE FIRST PRINCE OF WALES

His example was not forgotten. For by 1258 his grandson Llywelyn ap Gruffudd (Llywelyn the Last) had re-established Gwynedd's supremacy - and carried it a stage further, becoming the first Welsh ruler to claim the title 'Prince of Wales'. Nine years later, having successfully intervened in the civil wars between Henry III and rebel barons, his dominion over three-quarters of Wales was recognized by the Treaty of Montgomery. Only the remaining Marcher territories on the south coast and eastern borders now stood between Llywelyn and power over the whole land.

CASTLES OF CONFRONTATION

.lywelyn's clear ambition to complete ɪis conquest of Wales made him ›owerful enemies among the marchers. ʌs in his grandfather's time, they leployed the latest developments in nilitary technology against him, building astles defended by perimeters of nutually-supporting towers. Much the nost spectacular of these was Caerphilly Castle, where 'Red Gilbert' de Clare (d. 295) built the largest and strongest astle so far seen in Wales to defend his ordship of Glamorgan. Despite .lywelyn's pre-emptive strike against the ›art-built works, Caerphilly was quipped with a virtually impregnable ystem of concentric stone and water lefences. At their core was a castle omplete in itself, with a double circuit ›f walls and four gatehouses, one strong nough to serve as a self-contained keep.

Above: The strength and might of the threat posed by Llywelyn ap Gruffudd - Llywelyn the Last - can be gauged from the reaction of the Marcher lord, Gilbert de Clare, who responded with the construction of Caerphilly Castle. Caerphilly was the largest and strongest castle yet built in Wales and represented a considerable display of power by a single Marcher lord (Photograph by Skyscan).

THE LAST PRINCE

.lywelyn's final showdown with Gilbert de Clare ɪever materialized. Instead, he had to face the whole ›verwhelming might of England, led by its strong ɪew monarch Edward I. He fell in battle in 1282 at Cilmeri near Builth, where seven centuries later a nonument was raised to 'Llywelyn, Our Last Prince'. He was indeed to be the first, last and only Welsh uler of an independent Welsh nation: a nation soon o be bound with a chain of English castles.

Below: Dolforwyn Castle, Powys, overlooking the river Severn, near Montgomery. This is the only stronghold entirely built by Llywelyn ap Gruffudd, in defiance of commands to the contrary by King Edward I. Deliberately sited to rival the royal castle and borough at Montgomery, Llywelyn intended Dolforwyn to be a Welsh equivalent, with its own borough status and associated market.

Below Left: Some seven hundred years after the death of Llywelyn ap Gruffudd, this memorial stone to 'Llywelyn, Our Last Prince' was erected at Cilmeri, near Builth.

A CHAIN OF CASTLES

In July 1277, King Edward I unleashed against Wales the largest military force yet seen in nedieval Britain. Llywelyn ap Gruffudd had no lternative but to surrender to Edward's 'mercy', vhich left him only a reduced Gwynedd and the now mpty title of 'Prince of Wales'. Determined to revent a resurgence of Llywelyn's power, Edward emmed in his remaining lands with new fortresses. To the south, royal castles were built at Aberystwyth nd Builth; to the east, royal fortresses rose at Flint, Ruthin and Rhuddlan, reinforced by a new Marcher tronghold at Hawarden.

Incorporating the latest developments in military echnology, the new castles were master-minded by he brilliant architect James of St George, and built y armies of conscripted English labourers. In 1282, owever the part-built strongholds came under ttack. The Welsh had risen in nation-wide revolt gainst Edward's oppressive rule.

THE CHAIN EXTENDED: THE CASTLES OF 1282-83

The bitter fifteen-month campaign that followed ncluded some early Welsh successes. But in December 1282 Prince Llywelyn fell in a skirmish, nd in June 1283 his brother Dafydd was captured nd sent for brutal execution. Independent Wales lay rostrate at Edward's feet, and he was already nsuring that it would never rise again.

The heartlands of Llywelyn's principality were nnexed directly to the English crown, leaving the emainder of the country to the Marchers. To 'put n end finally to the malice of the Welsh' - Edward's wn words - he then added nine more links to his hain, extending it all round Gwynedd. New Marcher castles at Holt, Chirk and Denbigh, and efurbished Welsh strongholds at Dolwyddelan, Hope and Castell y Bere, backed up three xceptionally strong royal fortresses at Conwy, Caernarfon and Harlech.

This second campaign of castle building was an outstanding achievement, unequalled since the days of Rome. Even larger workforces marched - often under armed escort to prevent desertion - from every English shire, while English taxpayers and Italian moneylenders were wrung to finance Edward's stamp of power on conquered Wales. It would be proclaimed most stridently of all by his fortress-palaces at Conwy and Caernarfon.

eft: Harlech Castle, Gwynedd, built between 1283 and 1289, was et another link in Edward I's ever tightening chain of castles urrounding the heartlands of Gwynedd. The castle itself, although ompact, is concentrically built and perfectly tailored to the rocky utcrop from where it dominates the surrounding terrain.

A FINAL SOLUTION?

Though collectively the most impressive of all power symbols in medieval Britain, the practical effectiveness of Edward's astronomically expensive castles is open to question. They certainly did not deter a minor Welsh rising in 1287, or a more serious one in 1294-95, when the unfinished fortifications of Caernarfon were burnt and the king himself was virtually besieged at Conwy. This rebellion prompted a last link in the chain of castles: Beaumaris on Anglesey, the largest and most technically perfect of James of St George's 'concentric fortresses'. Begun in 1295, it was never finished - despite its architect's plea that 'Welshmen are Welshmen, and you have to watch out for them'. Just over a century later, the burgesses, bishops and barons of 'conquered' Wales would have cause to remember his warning.

1277	Edward I begins English conquest of Wales.
1282 - 83	Second war of English conquest: Llywelyn killed, and Welsh independence extinguished.
1277 - about **1300**	Chain of castles built to hold down conquered Wales.
1301	First English 'Prince of Wales' officially created.

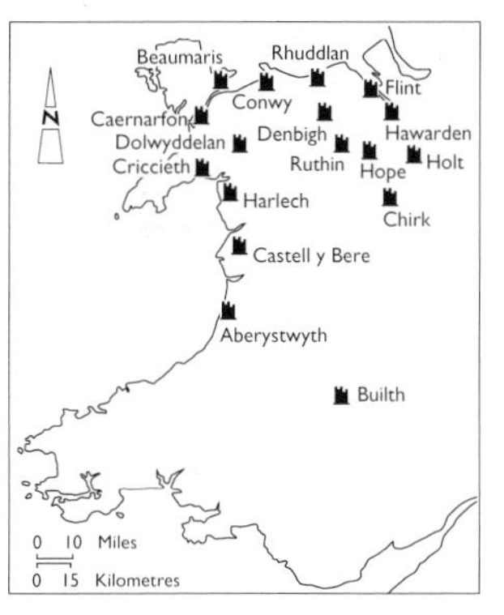

Map of English Castles of the Edwardian Campaigns in Wales

Left: Beaumaris Castle, Anglesey, was the last and largest of the castles built by Edward I in Wales. It was begun in 1295, following the revolt of Madog ap Llywelyn, and may have been intended as Edward's ultimate symbol of power over Wales. But events elsewhere soon beckoned Edward away from Wales, and the castle was never completed.

EDWARD I: THE PROPAGANDA OF POWER

Above: *King Edward I from a thirteenth-century manuscript (By permission of the British Library, Cotton Ms. Vitellius A XIII, f. 6v).*

Among the most warlike of English medieval monarchs, Edward I (1272-1307) was obsessed with '*legalitas*' - the enforcement of legal rights, especially his own. It was Llywelyn's hesitation to acknowledge him as rightful overlord which prompted Edward's first attack on Wales in 1277, and righteous indignation at 'treasonable' Welsh rebellion which fuelled his determination to finally subjugate Wales after 1282.

The symbolism of power was clearly very important to Edward, leading him to systematically destroy or carry off the royal regalia of defeated Gwynedd. He ate from plate made from Llywelyn's silver and melted down his seals of office; displayed his princely coronet in Westminster Abbey and paraded his holiest relics through London - where another trophy, Llywelyn's severed head, was also put on show. Even Aberconwy Abbey - the burial place of Llywelyn the Great and his family - had to be removed to make way for Conwy Castle, originally intended as Edward's own palace in Wales.

Meanwhile, Edward was keen to publicize his supposed links with more ancient rulers of Wales. He held an 'Arthurian' feast and tournament to celebrate his Welsh victories, and probably stage-managed the 'discovery' of the alleged body of the Emperor Maximus at Caernarfon.

Caernarfon Castle itself, built around a deliberately preserved Norman 'motte' and close to the Roman fort of *Segontium*, ostentatiously embodied Edward's claim to be both the successor of the Norman conquerors and the true heir of Imperial Rome. For its eagle-crowned turrets recalled Welsh traditions about Maximus, while its colour-banded walls consciously imitated those of Constantinople, City of the Emperors.

In 1284, Edward carefully arranged for his son to be born within this symbolically sited fortress. Whether or not the baby was proclaimed 'Prince of Wales' at birth, he was certainly so created at Lincoln sixteen years later - when he may even have been crowned with Llywelyn's looted coronet. With an English prince's assumption of Llywelyn's title, Edward's seizure of power in the land of Wales was symbolically complete.

Right: *The Great Seal of Edward I, showing the king on horseback. The horse trappings are charged with the arms of England (Copyright: Public Record Office).*

Left: *Edward I creating his son, Edward of Caernarfon, the first English 'Prince of Wales' in 1301 (By permission of the British Library, Cotton Ms. Nero D II, f. 191v).*

Perhaps the most impressive of Edward's Welsh castles were the fortress-palaces at Conwy (*above*) and Caernarfon (*below*). In addition to their role as symbols of overt military oppression, they were intended to serve as accommodation for the royal entourage on its sojourns in Wales, and thus incorporated apartments commensurate with the status of the king and queen of England. At Caernarfon, Edward appears to have gone further in his attempt to subdue the spirit of Welsh nationality by allying himself to the traditions of Maximus - the Welsh Macsen Wledig. For here, the colour-banded walls emulated those of Constantinople, City of Emperors, and the eagle-crowned turrets recalled Welsh legends about Maximus.

A TURBULENT LAND

THE CONSOLIDATION OF CONQUEST

dward I's great castles did not stand alone, for to each of them was attached a fortified town or borough', designed to consolidate English power. Their inhabitants were English colonists, lured here by grants of cheap land and commercial privileges: Welshmen were emphatically second-lass citizens, forbidden to live within the walls but required to trade there.

During the uneasy aftermath of conquest, older towns like Chepstow, Carmarthen and Tenby also renewed their defences. So too did the hurchmen and Marcher barons who strengthened astles like Llawhaden and Kidwelly. As the threat of Welsh risings apparently receded, however, more omfortable residences came into fashion: the owners of Tretower Castle even felt confident nough to abandon their stronghold for an unfortified manor house nearby. Yet Welsh esentments smouldered beneath the surface, and the omparatively tranquil fourteenth century ended with the national revolt led by Owain Glyndŵr.

The seal of Owain Glyndŵr as independent 'Prince of Wales', about 1405. Glyndŵr is depicted bearing princely regalia, enthroned and coroneted against a backdrop of the royal lions of Llywelyn (By permission of the National Museum of Wales).

1300 - 30	English conquest consolidated.
1400 - about **1415**	Owain Glyndŵr's rising.
1420 onwards	Welsh gentry exercising local power.
1455 - 85	Wars of the Roses.
1485	Henry Tudor crowned king of England, but Welsh hopes deferred.

OWAIN GLYNDŴR

The prosperous, cultured and partly English-ducated squire of Glyndyfrdwy and Sycharth, Owain was also the descendant of three Welsh dynasties, marked out by bards as the prophesied aviour of his nation. At the very outset of his evolt in 1400, indeed, he declared himself 'Prince of Wales'. By 1403 he effectively controlled he countryside from Anglesey to Glamorgan, raiding the hated towns and besieging English garrisons in their isolated castles. Even the great Edwardian fortresses of Harlech and Aberystwyth surrendered to him in 1404, and at this zenith of his success, he held a Welsh parliament at Machynlleth. His great seal of this date depicts him in all the panoply of his princely power, enthroned and coroneted against a backdrop of the royal lions of Llywelyn.

Thereafter the tide began to turn against him: in 1409 his last stronghold fell to English heavy cannon, and in about 1415 (like Arthur and other legendary heroes) he simply disappeared. His long and bitterly-fought struggle for national independence left a legacy of devastation and even more oppressive racial laws, designed to prevent Welshmen from wielding power of any kind in their own land.

he castle at Sycharth, Powys, the seat of Owain Glyndŵr.

A gilt-bronze harness mounting, bearing the arms of Owain Glyndŵr. It was found at Harlech Castle which Glyndŵr successfully besieged in 1404 and held until 1408 or 1409 (By permisssion of the National Museum of Wales).

THE OPPORTUNISTS

Even before the revolt was over, however, Welshmen were again exercising control at local levels. For though nominal power in Wales belonged to English kings and nobles, these generally absent landlords

This fifteenth-century manuscript illustration shows Sir William Herbert (d. 1469) and his wife Anne Devereux, kneeling at the feet of King Edward IV. It was Sir William, rising to a position of great power and influence in south-east Wales during the 'Wars of the Roses', who transformed Raglan into a veritable palace in the 1460s (By permission of the British Library, Royal Ms. 18 D II, f. 6).

found it necessary to administer their estates through Welsh deputies - often men who had fought with them in the French wars.

Among the most successful of these soldier-opportunists was Sir William ap Thomas (d. 1445), veteran of Agincourt and founder of Raglan Castle. His son William Herbert (d. 1469) rose still higher in English royal service. Created earl of Pembroke in 1468, he was the first Welshman to enter the English peerage. Under the Yorkist King Edward IV he became effectively viceroy of Wales, celebrating his power by developing Raglan into the most magnificent fortress-palace in late medieval Britain.

The principal hallmarks of status in late medieval Wales, indeed, were fine buildings and splendid possessions - like the beautiful altarpiece

The ornate fifteenth-century gatehouse at Raglan Castle. French parallels for this elaborate design can be identified, which may well have inspired Sir William Herbert's plans for Raglan. By emulating contemporary European styles Sir William would have further reinforced his position as a man of power and wealth.

:ommissioned from the Flemish artist, Memling, by ›ir John Dwnn of Kidwelly (d. 1503). It incorporates ɔortraits of Sir John and his wife (the sister of Edward IV's best friend) proudly wearing Yorkist :ollars of suns and white roses. They are the earliest :eal likenesses of Welsh people which survive.

The centre panel of the Dwnn triptych - or altarpiece - which ncorporates portraits of Sir John Dwnn of Kidwelly and his wife. Only families of some status were able to commission such fine works of art (By courtesy of the National Gallery, London).

YORKISTS, LANCASTRIANS AND TUDORS

Welshmen fought on both sides in the Wars of the Roses, the dynastic struggle between Yorkists and Lancastrians for the crown of England. Like Sir John Dwnn, William Herbert of Raglan and his kinsman Roger Vaughan (d. 1471) of Tretower Court, supported the Yorkists, the two latter losing their ives in the process. Others, particularly in west Wales, pinned their hopes for national salvation on :he leading Welsh Lancastrians, Jasper Tudor d.1495) and his nephew Henry. Descendants of Llywelyn the Great's chief minister, the Tudors were ılso closely related to the Lancastrian King Henry VI. After King Henry's murder in 1471, indeed, Henry Tudor inherited the sole Lancastrian claim to :he throne of England.

When Henry landed in Pembrokeshire in 1485, ıe received enthusiastic Welsh support - including, eventually, that of Sir Rhys ap Thomas. Yet his coronation as King Henry VII of England (1485-1509) did not immediately produce the results Welshmen hoped for. Though proud enough of his Welsh descent to add the red dragon to his royal ırms, Henry was not secure enough on his throne to nake sweeping changes. Another fifty years would ɔass before Wales was granted legal equality with England, allowing its rising gentry to assume full ɔower in their land.

CONSPICUOUS CONSUMPTION: SIR RHYS AP THOMAS

Late medieval wielders of power were expected to display 'largesse' - translatable as 'conspicuous consumption' or, more prosaically, 'showing off'. One of its foremost Welsh exponents was Sir Rhys ap Thomas (1449-1525), the leading magnate of early Tudor south-west Wales. He owed his position largely to an astute piece of opportunism: after a circumspect delay and much hard bargaining for future rewards, he had joined Henry Tudor's march to victory at Bosworth in 1485.

The proceeds of Henry VII's favour added considerably to Sir Rhys's sizeable income from inherited estates. His properties included castles at Narberth, Newcastle Emlyn and Weobley, to which he added a fine porch block. But his principal residence was Carew Castle, where he built sumptuous new lodgings embellished with Tudor royal heraldry.

His most famous display of conspicuous consumption was the lavish tournament held at Carew in 1506, to celebrate his election as Knight of the Garter. Some 600 knights and gentlemen from all over Wales attended this five-day extravaganza of jousting, hunting, religious services and immensely ceremonious banquets.

Sir Rhys's Carew was also an important focus of culture, attracting bards who compared it to King Arthur's Court. Some of its splendid furnishings still survive.

He died in 1525, having carefully provided for his family and twelve illegitimate offspring. But six years later his heir fell victim to Henry VIII's suspicions, and the family estates were forfeited to the crown.

Above: *The tomb effigy of Sir Rhys ap Thomas (1449-1525) in St Peter's Church, Carmarthen.*

Top: *The porch block which Sir Rhys ap Thomas added to Weobley Castle.*
Below: *Sir Rhys's principal residence was here, at Carew Castle, where he built sumptuous new lodgings and held a long remembered tournament in 1506.*

Below: *Sir Rhys's 'Garter Chair' bearing his Garter arms (By permission of the National Museum of Wales, Welsh Folk Museum).*

THE TRIUMPH OF THE GENTRY

1536 - 43	'Acts of Union' make Wales a single unit and encourage rise of Welsh gentry.
1543 onwards	Welsh gentry building new mansions.
1642 - 48	Civil Wars: widespread destruction of castles.

Between 1536 and 1543, sweeping changes in Church and State radically altered the power-structure of Wales. The Protestant Reformation severed the Church's links with Rome, transferring much of its property to lay landowners. Still more important was the legislation - the so-called 'Acts of Union' - which abolished the medieval divisions between 'Principality' and 'Marches'. Thereby Wales assumed its modern form as a single unit, divided into counties and subject to English law. Legal discrimination against Welshmen was abandoned, and for the first time they were represented in Parliament. In effect, Wales was amalgamated with England.

This development was welcomed by most Welshmen, and in particular by the landowning Welsh gentry. Their way now lay open to influence as magistrates and members of parliament, and to wealth as courtiers or merchants. For the next two and a half centuries, the gentry would wield unrivalled power in the land.

Neath Abbey, where the Williams family proclaimed their newly-acquired gentry status by raising a splendid mansion over the shell of the abandoned monastic buildings.

NEW POWER, NEW MANSIONS

They proclaimed their status by building new mansions. Some, like those of the Williams family at Neath and the Mansels at Margam, were adapted from abandoned monasteries, but most were completely new foundations - like Gwernyfed in Powys, status-symbol of the wealthy self-made lawyer Sir David Williams. Though many Welsh gentry families boasted descent from princely

A detail from the highly ornate plasterwork at Plas Mawr, Conwy - the fashionable Flemish-style town house of the much-travelled Robert Wynn. This showy display of wealth reflects his new-found status as a rising star in the Tudor gentry of Wales.

he remarkably well-preserved izabethan house of Plas Mawr, onwy, which was inspired by e flourishing 'Renaissance' shions.

dynasties, indeed, most owed their rise to power to the talents of Tudor and Jacobean entrepreneurs like Sir Rice Mansel of Oxwich or Sir John Wynn of Gwydir (1553-1627), who founded his family's pre-eminence in north Wales.

Other Welshmen served abroad as courtiers, returning to build fashionable new 'Renaissance' mansions in their homeland. Flemish-style Plas Mawr in Conwy, home f the much-travelled Robert Wynn, is probably the nost remarkable and best-preserved Elizabethan own house in Britain, especially notable for laborate plasterwork. The showy Renaissance nansion of Plas Teg, Flintshire, was built by another ourtier, Sir John Trevor, while Sir Thomas Morgan's Ruperra, Caerphilly, followed the courtly ashion for sham 'castles'.

late seventeenth-century painting of Margam Old House and ardens. The dissolved abbey of Margam was purchased by Sir Rice Iansel who succeeded in elevating his family to the upper echelons Glamorgan society in the sixteenth century. Margam soon became e principal seat of the Mansels (Private collection: Photograph by e National Museum of Wales).

A DYNASTY OF GENTRY: THE MANSELS

Left: *Sir Rice Mansel (1487-1559) from his memorial tomb in the abbey church, Margam.* Centre: *Sir Rice's initials and the Mansel arms, quartered with those of the Scurlage and Penrice families, proclaim the family's ancestral claim to status above the gateway at Oxwich Castle.* Right: *Sir Rice's final recognition as a man of standing came in 1557 when, as this document records, Queen Mary granted him a licence to keep a personal retinue of fifty gentlemen (By courtesy of the National Library of Wales).*

Although the Mansels had owned Oxwich Castle and other property in Gower since the fourteenth century, the real founder of their fortunes was the able and energetic Sir Rice Mansel (1487-1559). The godson and namesake of Sir Rhys (Rice) ap Thomas (his father's cousin and patron) he initially attracted Henry VIII's favour by his naval and military exploits. After the Dissolution of the Monasteries, he was allowed to purchase the valuable estates of Margam Abbey, making him one of the greatest Glamorganshire landowners.

Like many other successful Welsh gentlemen, Sir Rice celebrated his prosperity by turning his ancestral home at Oxwich into an up-to-date mansion. But his enhanced rise in status under Queen Mary (1553-58) provoked the jealousy of older-established families like the Herberts, sparking off a notorious 'affray' at Oxwich in 1557.

Though less able than his father, Sir Rice's son Sir Edward Mansel (d. 1595) built even more lavishly at Oxwich, adding an impressive multi-storey range complete with fashionable long gallery. But under Sir Thomas (1556-1631) - the first Mansel baronet - the family seat was transferred to Margam Abbey, newly converted into a 'fair and sumptuous house' with elaborate pleasure-gardens.

Raised to the peerage as Barons Mansel of Margam in 1711, the family ranked among the powerful Georgian 'landed Titans' who dominated Welsh politics. Their main line died out in 1750, whereafter their descendant Christopher Rice Mansel Talbot (1803-90) followed prevailing fashion by building the immense sham-Gothic 'Margam Castle' to replace Margam Abbey.

A magnificent portrait of Sir Thomas (1556-1631) - the first Mansel baronet - and his wife (By permission of the National Museum of Wales).

The elegant Tudor windows at Carew Castle mark the position of Sir John Perrot's enormous long gallery in the new wing he added to the castle late in the sixteenth century (By courtesy of the Wales Tourist Board).

CASTLES INTO COUNTRY HOUSES

Real castles, indeed, retained something of their status as symbols of continuing power. Though many fell into ruin during the long Tudor and early Stuart peace, some were expensively updated in the new Renaissance style. Thus Sir John Perrot (d. 1592) - allegedly an illegitimate son of Henry VIII - added a magnificent new wing to Carew Castle, including an enormous 'long gallery'. Such galleries were an indispensable element of aristocratic Elizabethan mansions. One of the finest survives at Powis Castle, constructed in 1592-93 during Sir Edward Herbert's conversion of the medieval fortress into a luxurious country house.

The most splendid of all Welsh 'country-house castles' was Raglan. There the earls of Worcester reconstructed the medieval fortress-palace during the second half of the sixteenth century: its new long gallery, banqueting hall and other fashionable appurtenances left visitors in no doubt that this was the home of the wealthiest and most powerful family in south Wales.

THE DESTRUCTION OF THE CASTLES

On the outbreak of Civil War between king and parliament in 1642, however, Raglan and other Welsh castles abruptly reverted to their original military role. Dilapidated fortresses from Beaumaris to Chepstow were hurriedly repaired, and Pembroke and Harlech were among those that endured long sieges. They paid heavily for their last hour of glory as powers in the land. For many were badly damaged in the fighting, and after Parliament's victory more were 'slighted' or partially demolished - often with considerable difficulty. Raglan's Great Tower, having defied besieging artillery and worn out demolition gangs, required laborious undermining before it 'fell down in a lump'.

Henceforward, the elegant mansions of the aristocracy and gentry would reign unrivalled as symbols of wealth and influence in Wales.

The splendid long gallery at Powis Castle, constructed by Sir Edward Herbert in 1592-93, during the conversion of the medieval fortress into a luxurious country house (By courtesy of the Wales Tourist Board).

LANDED TITANS

The east front of Erddig, showing part of the formal gardens created by John Meller between 1718 and 1733. Meller was a London lawyer who had purchased Erddig from Joshua Edisbury in 1716 when the latter was declared bankrupt and unable to finance his ambitious plans for the house and gardens. Wealth had now become the means to wield power in the landscape (By courtesy of the Wales Tourist Board).

After the upheavals of Civil War and Cromwellian rule, the Welsh gentry marked the restoration of ing Charles II and stability by replacing war-amaged mansions. Great Castle House at Ionmouth succeeded ruined Raglan, while burnt-ıt Abbey Cwm Hir in Powys was replaced by a odest residence at nearby Devannor.

The distribution of power among the gentry, owever, had begun to shift - as demonstrated by redegar House, the largest and grandest estoration mansion in south Wales. It was built etween 1664 and 1672 by the Morgans, one of the lect band of great families which steadily increased eir wealth during the later Stuart and Georgian eriods. Such 'insatiable Leviathans' inexorably vallowed up the estates and local influence of their sser neighbours, concentrating power into the ands of fewer and fewer families. The symbols of eir dominance were enormous country houses, hich only they could afford to build.

Joshua Edisbury, indeed, bankrupted himself by eginning Erddig, near Wrexham, leaving it to be ompleted by a London lawyer. Elsewhere, too, milies of English or Scots origin - like the Talbots ıd the Butes - took over the estates of ancient 'elsh families which failed to produce male heirs.

ne richly furnished saloon at Chirk Castle - particularly notable r its ornately carved and gilded panel mouldings - was mmissioned by the Myddletons to demonstrate that the family ıd lost none of its power or status over time (By courtesy of the 'ales Tourist Board).

THE POWER OF FASHION

y far the wealthiest of all the Georgian 'landed itans', admittedly, were the Wynns of Wynnstay, ear Ruabon, Wrexham, descendants of Welsh rinces and Elizabethan entrepreneurs. Their lesser counterparts around Aberystwyth were the Powells, who in 1739 built Nanteos - 'the nightingales brook' in the new Italianate style. Keeping up with such changing fashions was an important indicator of continuing power, and the owners of older houses could not afford to be left behind. Thus the Herberts added an immense new ballroom and picture gallery to Powis Castle, while the Myddletons of Chirk Castle commissioned a suite of 'state rooms' in the latest Classical mode.

GARDENS OF THE GREAT

Such rooms could be viewed only by a chosen few: but the surroundings of great houses trumpeted the power and wealth of their owners to a much wider audience. Exotic walled gardens like those of seventeenth-century Llannerch or Margam Abbey were extended into the countryside by tree-lined avenues miles long, focused on eye-catching summer houses. Vast formal parklands like those of Erddig and Chirk Castle were proclaimed to admiring travellers by imposing gateways and stylish roadside lodges, while more privileged visitors were struck dumb by Margam's famous orangery, still the largest in Britain.

Towards the end of the eighteenth century, studied formality gave way to a fashion for rearranging whole landscapes to conform with their

1660	Restoration of King Charles II
about **1670- 1770**	Great landowners monopolize power. Heyday of country house.
about **1770**	Beginning of Industrial Revolution in Wales.

SIR WATKIN WILLIAMS WYNN

The portrait of Sir Watkin Williams Wynn (left), with friends, painted by Pompeo Batoni, when Wynn visited Rome on his 'Grand Tour' in 1748 (By permission of the National Museum of Wales).

Sir Watkin Williams Wynn of Wynnstay (1748-89) succeeded at the age of five months to a baronetcy and the greatest of all Welsh landed estates. Indeed, he was one of the wealthiest men in Britain, well able to celebrate his coming of age with a banquet for 15,000 guests and to become the most generous patron of the arts Wales has ever produced.

His portrait, painted by Pompeo Batoni when he visited Rome on a cultural 'Grand Tour', reflects the breadth of his interests. His friends included Sir Joshua Reynolds and Handel, David Garrick the actor and Robert Adam the architect. Adam designed his London town house, as well as a 153 piece silver table service for its 'Eating Room' and a great silver-gilt Classical punchbowl to commemorate his wins at Chester Races.

Sir Watkin also professed a deep interest in Welsh antiquities and 'bardic' traditions: Chief President of the Cymmrodorion Society, he liked to appear dressed as a Druid at London masquerades. He employed a harper at Wynnstay, built a playhouse there, and munificently assisted Welsh scholars, musicians and painters.

But he also demanded an absolute monopoly of power in his Welsh 'kingdom', where his agents shamelessly bullied and intimidated voters at parliamentary elections. Even his immense landed income could not match his outlay: in the end he dared not visit Wales for fear of creditors, and he died heavily in debt.

Right: *A silver-gilt dessert service designed by Robert Adam for Sir Watkin Williams Wynn (By permission of the National Museum of Wales).*

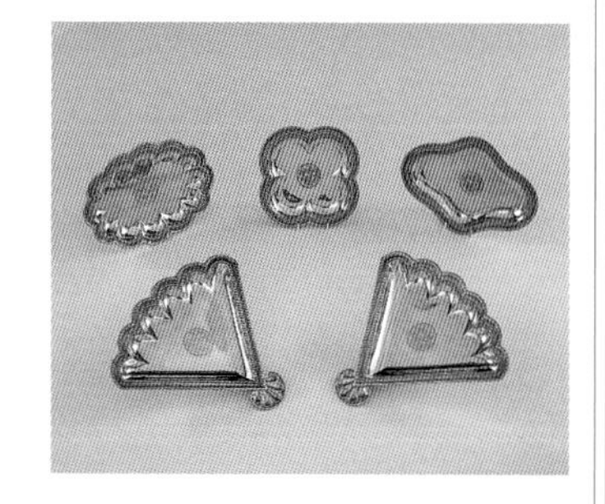

Below Right: *In 1771 Robert Adam designed this Classical silver-gilt punchbowl to commemorate Williams Wynn's wins at Chester races (By permission of the National Museum of Wales).*

Below: *The Williams Wynn toilet service, commissioned from Thomas Heming in London, on the occasion of Sir Watkin's marriage to his first wife, Lady Henrietta Somerset, fifth daughter of the fourth duke of Beaufort (By permission of the National Museum of Wales).*

The magnificent wrought-iron gates at Chirk were designed and made for the Myddleton family by Robert and Thomas Davies of Bersham, between 1719 and 1721. The family arms adorn the gates and two wolves - which feature in the heraldry - top the gate piers to either side (By courtesy of the Wales Tourist Boar

owner's concept of suitably tamed nature. If a genuine 'romantic' ruin like Dinefwr Castle or Valle Crucis Abbey could be incorporated into the pictur so much the better: if not, one could always be buil and even provided with a paid 'Druidic' hermit.

Thus the surroundings of Plas Newydd in Anglesey were redesigned for the earl of Uxbridge, who had also recently remodelled his mansion in Gothic style. Much of the immense expense of hous and landscaping was met from the proceeds of copper mining on Uxbridge's estates, managed for him by the 'Copper King' Thomas Williams of Llanidan. An ambitious but plain-dealing Anglesey solicitor, 'Twm Chwarae Teg' (Tom Fairplay) had cornered the British copper market by 1790. Men like Williams and Uxbridge - entrepreneurs and aristocrats - would together dominate the booming new Wales of the Industrial Revolution.

Right: This painting of about 1662 gives a bird's-eye view of the once spectacular gardens built on the terraces below the house at Llannerch, Denbighshire. The gardens, complete with walled enclosures and exotic water tricks, were an ostentatious extensio to the house as well as a very conspicuous display of wealth. Alas, they were destroyed in the Victorian period and now lie buried beneath the turf (By kind permission of Yale Center for British Ar Paul Mellon Collection).

ENTREPRENEURS AND ARISTOCRATS

1790	Industrial Revolution in Wales gathers pace.
1830	Maximum iron production at Merthyr Tydfil.
1890	Cardiff the largest port in the world.
1913	Peak of Welsh coal production.
1914 - 18	First World War, 40,000 Welshmen killed.
1920s onwards	Break-up of aristocratic estates.
1930 onwards	Heavy industry in decline.

Above Right: Industry fuelled the power of a handful of wealthy entrepreneurs in Wales during the nineteenth century. The Crawshays were one such family, whose ironworks at Merthyr Tydfil provided sufficient profits to build the neo-Gothic mansion of Cyfarthfa Castle. This painting of the scene inside the casthouses at the Crawshay's Cyfarthfa ironworks is a reminder of the sharp contrast between the lives of those who wielded power and those who laboured under its tyranny (By permission of Cyfarthfa Castle Museum, Merthyr Tydfil).

Between 1770 and 1914, Wales underwent the most dramatic changes in its recorded history. It was transformed from a largely agricultural land with about 500,000 inhabitants into a predominantly industrial nation of over 2.1 million people, overwhelmingly concentrated in the south and south-east. The population of one coalfield parish there - Bedwellte - leapt by 1,795 per cent in fifty years. The raw materials of the new Wales were copper, lead, slate, iron and coal - and labour. Its rulers were the entrepreneurs who exploited them, and the landowners on whose estates they were found.

THE RICH MAN IN HIS CASTLE

These mineral barons adopted the power-symbols of a romanticized medieval past, enthusiastically following the fashion for neo-Gothic 'castles'. At Penrhyn near Bangor, the slate-rich Pennants entertained their guests in a massive 'Norman fortress' begun in 1820. From Cyfarthfa Castle - raised in a single year by armies of labourers - the 'Iron King' William Crawshay overlooked (and sought to overawe) the booming Merthyr Tydfil ironworks established by his grandfather, a self-made Yorkshire tycoon who became one of Britain' first millionaires.

But it was coal which powered Industrial Revolution Wales, and which became its most profitable resource. By the 1890s Cardiff was the largest port in the world, exporting millions of tons a year through the docks founded by the second marquess of Bute.

Right: Cardiff docks in about 1860. Developed by the second marquess of Bute early in the nineteenth century, the docks continued to flourish, and by the 1890s Cardiff had become the premier port of the world, exporting millions of tons of coal (By permission of the National Museum of Wales, Welsh Industrial and Maritime Museum).

THE MARQUESSES OF BUTE

John, the second marquess of Bute (1793-1848), 'the founder of modern Cardiff', whose development of the docks consolidated the Bute family fortune and status. A portrait, taken from an original, by E. Trevor Haynes, about 1866.

The second marquess of Bute (1793-1848) combined the resources of a great landowner with the skills of a far-seeing entrepreneur. Having inherited the Glamorgan estates of the Welsh Herbert family - including Cardiff Castle and much of the coal-rich Rhondda valley - he was not content merely to accept a share in their exploitation by others. Instead he took on their management himself, pioneering new mining techniques and above all investing in new docks at Cardiff to handle the coal they produced. His efforts left his son one of the world's richest men.

The third marquess of Bute (1847-1900) was the antithesis of his hard-headed father. Scholar and recluse, psychic researcher and Roman Catholic convert, he shared his vision of recreating the medieval past with his brilliant but eccentric architect William Burges. Between 1867 and 1881 they realized it at Cardiff Castle.

Though its towered and pinnacled exterior made some attempt at historical accuracy, the interior of their dream-palace gave free rein to Burges's exuberant creativity. This attained zeniths of fantasy in apartments like the Summer Smoking Room and the Arab Room with its golden 'Islamic' roof.

Not content with Cardiff Castle, in 1875 Bute and Burges turned to nearby Castell Coch. Founded by 'Red Gilbert' de Clare in the thirteenth century, this was almost totally rebuilt as Bute's 'occasional summer residence'. A fairytale castle in the woods, its drawing room ceiling is thronged with painted birds, and every detail of its furnishing reflects the medieval fantasy theme. Rarely used and scarcely altered, it preserves its creators' vision unchanged.

John Patrick Crichton Stuart, third marquess of Bute (1847-1900), as mayor of Cardiff, 1890-91 (By kind permission of the marquess of Bute).

Above: *The splendid vaulted drawing room ceiling in Castell Coch, where great gold ribs fall amongst birds, butterflies and stars in the sky.*

Right: *The Summer Smoking Room in the Clock Tower at Cardiff Castle. A bronze model of the world, set in tiles, is inlaid in the centre of the floor, and the large chandelier represents the sun. Beautiful hand-painted tiles on the wall illustrate classical themes.*

Castell Coch, built 1875 - the lavish symbol of a rich man's dream - overlooks the modern city of Cardiff. The city's docks proved the source of much of the Bute's wealth and power in the nineteenth century.

Blaenavon Ironworks, once a flourishing iron-making complex at the heart of the Welsh Industrial Revolution, was designated part of the Blaenavon Industrial Landscape World Heritage Site in 2000. The site is in the care of Cadw: Welsh Historic Monuments, to be fully conserved and preserved for future generations as a vital record, and memorial, of Wales's past industrial triumphs.

A LAND IN TRANSITION

When Lord Bute died in 1900, the days of the aristocrats and entrepreneurs were numbered. Great landowners had lost their monopoly of parliamentary power, and after the First World War many of their estates would be broken up, passing at last to the men who actually farmed them. Their enormous country houses, impossible to maintain or to staff, were all too often abandoned or demolished. Then the narrowly-based industrial economy created by the entrepreneurs began its long decline, as markets for coal and steel shrank or shifted focus. The Industrial Revolution has now become part of the history of Wales.

Chieftains in their hillforts, princes and barons in their castles, aristocrats and industrialists in their mansions, have all in turn wielded power in the land. Today Wales is a nation in transition; who their successors are, or will be, remains an open question.